The Ugly Generation

Poems by FEO

The Ugly Generation

By
Feo

Edited by
David Misialowski

ISBN
978-1-944854-14-0

 **www.poodpawprints.com**
facebook.com/poodpawprints
youtube.com/@poodpawprints
instagram.com/poodpawprints

The Ugly Generation, Published by Pood Paw Prints, 18819 71st ave NE, Kenmore WA 98028, United States. This book copyright 2024 FEO and Pood Paw Prints. All rights reserved. No portion of this product may be reproduced or transmitted, by any form or by any means, without the express written permission of FEO or Pood Paw Prints.

For the ghosts of the mentally insane, my thoughts are with you.

Margaux T.

The world is so different without the fog
A compliment is self inflicted
The cobble hill phantom has gone missing
Ultra has vanished
The snow is now marble
The bishops cannot defend the mourning pawns — seekers of piety
Altering the state of consciousness
Cold in the open casket
Creation of the lost zodiac
Spit fire on the disposed
A lustful howl at the crescent moon
Blood-orange night sky
The menstrual painting finished in the white stone church
Parallel crucifix
Bishops losing faith
A silhouette facing the glass canvas
There are love poems in those eyes
Only a rose can die with dignity.

Have You Seen This Man?

He used to walk down Delancey with a smile for the day.
Saying hello to the men who sold the leather jackets on the street.
The locals would wave back as he waved to them every morning.
A homeless man by the pizzeria couldn't wait to see him, because the man would always give him money to buy a slice.
The whole neighborhood knew him. He had a heart of gold.
He smiled and waved goodbye every evening as he headed back home.
No one knew anything about him — where he lived, if he took a train home. No one even knew his name. No one had thought to ask.
But things would change past Grand St.
for some reason it always rained there
and he always forgot to have an umbrella
he walked past the odors of rotten vegetables that consumed him
it always smells on Grand St
and it always rained
and it would always be cold in the mornings
the streets were never kept up, not even the buildings
this was the way he got home at nights, and no one would notice.
he would walk into his room and throw the keys on the floor
there was only one light on and it was in the restroom and he hated it in there because of the mirror
he would turn the shower head on and wash his hair and shave the hair off his body to feel more clean from his walk back
the light would flicker off and on and his legs would bleed from the shaving
he covered the mirror with newspapers and drank tap water from a dirty mug
he'd lay on his floor and rock himself back and forth to

sooth his aching bones, and he would bite his nails till they bled
the entire room was covered with mold, the blankets as well
no one ever heard of him
they only witnessed him
only the people of Delancey knew of him
have you seen him?

The 10th of April.

**The fog had taken over New York
the freedom tower wasn't visible and the tunnel exit didn't appear
Tudor city was missing
the FDR had phantom cars
several buses to Newark but no travelers
unattached in the fog of midtown
Grand Central was as dead as Greenwood cemetery
cemetery weather
funerals too
mother's birthday.**

4-5-15

I don't like this poem. So I won't write it.

Oro

Mott St spring time go happy time
the elder christian below the cross
a tree that protects the holy spirit
a reef of Mary, an asexual woman
Broome St happy times
hoof prints on the sidewalk
hours from now I'll be with old friends
my comfort zone
watching the big hand
standing on the basement gate that's half open
please return to oro.

Sex

Urinating in front of me first, then she stood up and removed her panties
the scent of sex was overwhelming
she pulled up her dress and placed her hands against the wall
my erection rubbed against her till I reached for her gash and stuck it in
she sank her face in the sink and I went deeper
she was dripping, so was I
I ran my fingers up and down her back and went in deeper
pulled out and let her taste me, just in time because someone knocked on the door
the scent of sex went with us as we left the restroom
we parted ways on the streets
and never spoke again.

4-2-15.

Went to see the band The Damned, where I bought a beret. Got in the middle of the crowd and yelled out "DO WHATEVER YOU WANT TO ME." And they did.

I was the plaything and I liked it.

It began to rain outside of the venue where I saw The Damned.

The Punks got pissed.

The violence hit the streets.

And I liked it.

Went to a bar after the show where I saw The Damned and bought a beret.

Met a Punk girl who saw The Damned where I bought a beret. We went somewhere private.

She was wet. And I liked it

In the rain I saw The Damned and I bought a beret and got into the middle of the Punks and yelled "DO WHATEVER YOU WANT TO ME." And they did.

The dirty gems.

An
 all-girl riot.
Beautiful punk girls. Just like my old days.
Marisa has the best guitar face. I love it when she screams.
Music from my past. Who needs another Jesus holiday
when you got that?

Schizophrenic one night stand.

Benzos — that's her thing
Meth — used to it
On her own since she was a little girl
She hears things, she always does
Every twitch is a different drug
And every voice is a different drink
Why are all the crazy ones taken?
It's always the pretty ones that are crazier than me. But I get it
People with disorders make great lovers
The voices in their heads scream louder in bed
We can be paranoid together if you'd let me.

Jimmy the Swede vs the city of New York.

Jimmy's always crazy. He's the only man who would challenge the world and rent out his apartment at the same time

**Jimmy has written about prostitutes and like an idiot he fell for them
but that's what makes him Jimmy**

a poet who loves America more than anyone

the people vs Jimmy.

#4-21-15.

**Did not want to write the day before. Just wouldn't be
respectful
of course a poet should always be that way
love comes first you know. The best reason to smile
a happy face
wearing black forever
every day a eulogy.**

Absolutely.

I could have had you, but we wouldn't have remembered. We were drunk at the time. We kissed and took photos. We made out next to the Guatemalan flag on the wall that was torn down by drunken passion.
Thoughtful that you didn't want me to smell your period stain, but I don't mind. I like the taste of blood.

The Back Is Closed.

It has come to many people's attention that we are entering a new decade
Many have reflected on what the last 10 years were like
Some have asked what the last 10 years of my life have been
I blocked it out. But remember some
From beginning to end of the last decade

I became an adult,
I survived the recession,
I've seen the city change,
I got a cheap haircut,
I became an addict,
I became a heavy smoker,
I got the Bellevue blues,
I visited the place of my birth, and never spoke to the extended family ever again,
I lost my heart,
I slept on park benches,
I've slept in the basements of past establishments,
I became medicated,
I was homeless,
I discovered love,
I became an artist,
I became an ink stain,
I became New York,
I met my heroes,
I lost heroes,
I made friends,
I lost friends,
Some moved,
Some lost touch,
Some died,
I still cry in public,
I continue to figure it out,
I'm still surviving.

Downtown 6 train to Bleeker.

Bleeker St in the afternoon
Street walkers
Street shoppers
Beggars and street maps. Food cart vendors, north of Houston sometimes
Lafayette train stops and used books
Cab drivers praying and not giving a damn
Provocative photos
Smokers on broadway and the homeless dancers
Jewelry and fake diamonds on Prince St
A tea shop
White fur coats and black leather gloves
If I were a millionaire I would buy all of this for you.
That's because I miss everything
There's a poet in Soho.

Staycation lonesome.

The warmth from the summer comes into my apt and I wake up sweaty in the same Fred Perry shirt from 3 days before, and yet I somehow managed to take off one boot

The small window in my kitchen lets in a beautiful natural light, enough to light my space

When you work very hard for 3 years straight it becomes difficult to learn how to take it easy

Time off is a personal insane asylum. You don't know what to do with yourself.

Rehab.

**Boozed and tattered
sweaty and shaky
the runs on the run
breaking of the teeth
losing it
high on whiskey
high on vaginal sex and sloppy masturbation.**

For Rent.

Please go to the future sight of our Avenue A residential renting high rise

Luxuries include an office style living space

A 24-hour front desk man who will cater to your every postal delivery request

A living room view of future residential and commercial buildings

Each floor will have one low-income renter to give off a "real urban" vibe for the other residents.

A sit down with satan.

F - I would like to thank you for taking the time to speak with me. I know that you're a busy man, so I'll come out with it.

I want to sell it to you, in exchange of a simpler life.

I know what I'm getting involved in. And I'm fine with it. Your call.

S - Listen I'm going to be honest with you, there's nothing I can really do with it.

F - Oh. Are you sure?

S - Yup.

F - Oh. All right then. What should I do in the meantime?

S - Just continue what you're doing.

F - Cool. Thanks anyways guy.

I Spy

I spy with my little eye something beginning with "A"
Atmosphere, atmospheric
I spy with my little eye something beginning with "B"
Beauty, being
I spy with my little eye something beginning with "C"
Caring, concerned
I spy with my little eye something beginning with "F"
Forgiving
I spy with my little eye something beginning with "G"
Giving
I spy with my little eye something beginning with "K"
Kiss
I spy with my little eye something beginning with "L"
Love
I spy with my little eye something beginning with "P"
Pure
I spy with my little eye something beginning with "F"
Forever.

Mind yourself.

It's miserable out, love it
a great day to lie in a dark room and think about life
what you have, how lucky you are to be alive
the people that you know
family
friends
mortality
saying goodbye to yourself in the rain
parting ways forever
without an umbrella
wishing you can say goodbye in French because it's more romantic
rainy days are perfect for resurrections
jours de pluie.

Saw Dust.

      As I lift the blue rag of bar vomit that drips on to my shoes
      and the clunk noise of empty beer and liquor bottles I am reminded of the only goal I have, taking out the trash
      Watching the basement stairs bleed of garbage reminds me of last year
      The year the world shut down. I tried to shut myself down. But alas, as does the garbage that I carry over my shoulders keeps existing, so do I
      But you stick your tongue at me grim reaper. And show off the souls of my friends and family that you have claimed
      A tip of the hat grim reaper. I'll meet you for a game of chess
      In Brooklyn I can see the sun rise. It gives me a sense of hope
      Shall I beat you to it?
      Saw dust and wrist cuts.

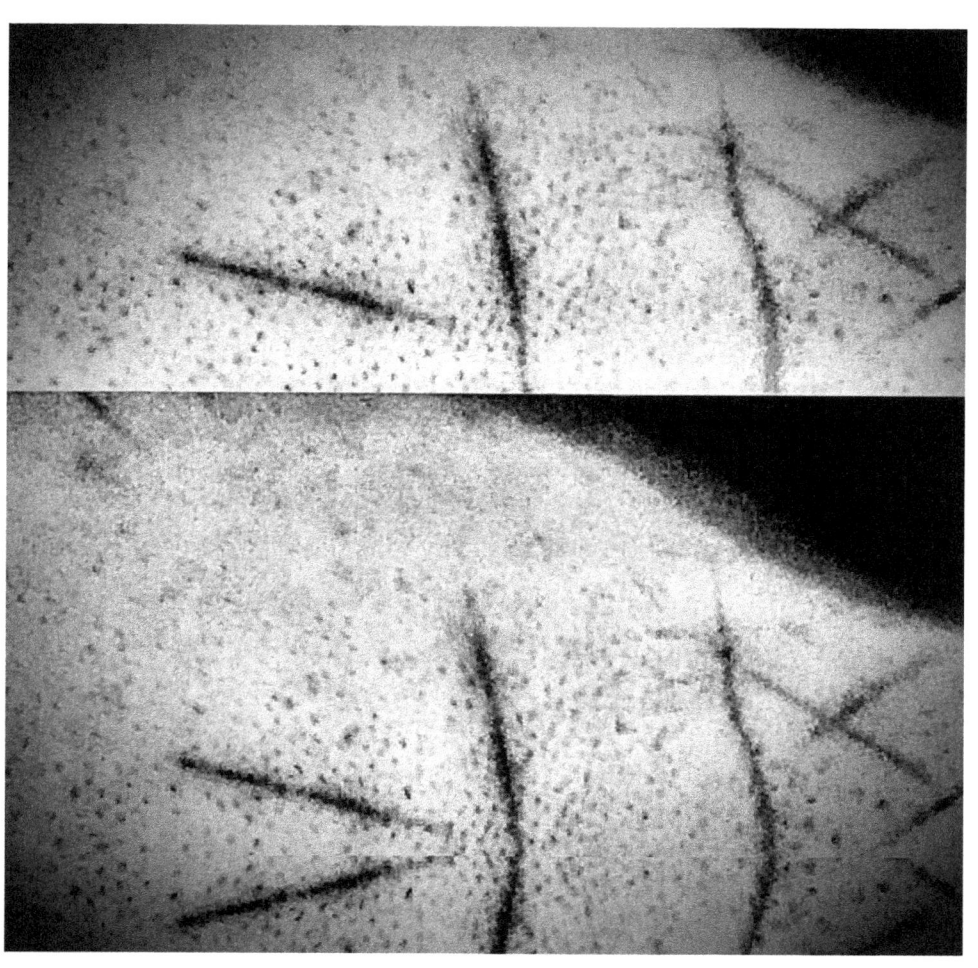

Drip.

      Drip Drip Drip From my kitchen sink
      Drip Drip Drip
      From the pipes at the train station of the 4 5 6
      Drip Drip Drip Junkie tar
      Drip Drip Drip Labor, thoughts, and tears that fall on the bar
      Drip Drip Drip Addiction bound
      Drip Drip Drip
      Waiting for the body to shut down
      Drip Drip

Lunch with a wiseguy.

Entering a luncheonette in the Lower East Side I was greeted by a lovely woman with freckles and braided hair.

She sat me at the counter and threw me a menu. I ordered my usual and my attention was arrested by a man behind the counter on the phone.

His was talking to someone on the phone while screaming out the orders to the kitchen: TURKEY CLUB NO TOMATOES!! CHEESEBURGER DELUXE WITH A SIDE OF MAYO!! To me he said, GIVE ME 15 MINUTES BUDDY!!

I was intrigued with him. He didn't have time to give change to a crazy woman who wanted a coffee for a dollar, because he had calls to receive and orders to give.

The lovely woman with freckles brought me my food. I heard the sound of a ringing phone. It just rang and rang. It was coming from a black phone next to the white one that the New York screamer was using to take orders.

The loud man grabbed the black phone and yelled out, LUNCHEONETTE HOW CAN I HELP YOU!! Then he said in a soft voice that only I could hear: "Yeah he's here, hang on let me get him." HEY ANTHONY!! IT'S ... for you.
He was screaming at a table where four men sat. One very built man stood up and headed toward the counter.

He walked behind it and grabbed the phone and turned his back to the window and said, "It's all settled, Peter. You don't have to worry about it."

The joint was loud but my curiosity got the better of me. All I could see was his smile reflected in the window of the luncheonette. He spoke for a few more seconds, and then handed the phone back to the loud man.

He was walking back to his table when he noticed me. The whole joint was still, except for him.

He had a certain look in his eyes as he stared me down.

He knew I had heard his conversation. He knew I wasn't stupid. He walked past me and patted me on the back and headed back to his crew.

I waved down the pretty freckle-faced woman for my check. The meal was 8 bucks and I gave her 40 dollars. I told her to keep the change for my order, and give the rest to Anthony. Tell him that his lunch was on me.

An ugly poem.

This is not a Bukowski poem
There's no horse tracks here or empty bottles of wine
There's no California coast, just east coast pollution
no fights outside of bars
no smelly old men
no sympathy for writing
no Polacks or Germans
I never grew up in Cali, we've had this conversation before
wasn't suppose to come here, just stepped in
heh, you old fool
just like the rest of them.

Maya.

A man woke up in a state of panic to the sound of an alarm from his phone. He reached for it to turn it off. He got up fully dressed from the night before and turned the light on in his kitchen and reached for a bottle of pills. His hands shook as he poured himself a glass of water. He washed down the pills with the water, and immediately began to feel calmer. He sat on the edge of his bed and pulled on a pair of red boots. He grabbed a bag on the floor next to his bed and looked inside to see that he still had a stack of papers and a roll of tape in the bag. Rubbing his eyes, he grabbed his coat and bag and left his darkened studio apartment.

The same morning a young woman left her apartment building with her backpack, heading for the local bodega to order a cup of coffee. Her phone rang, and she answered it. "Hello? Oh hey. No, I haven't figured out what to do for my final project. I did write something but I wasn't happy with it. Listen, I'm on my way to get coffee and then school. I'll talk to you later. Bye."

As she left the bodega with her coffee she walked alongside a park. When she stopped by a trash can to throw away her finished cup of coffee, something caught her eye. A piece of paper with writing on it was taped to the can. Investigating, she discovered that it was a poem, titled but unsigned. She read it quickly, and then threw away her empty cup. She kept the poem and hurried toward the subway station.

While walking, she noticed another poem taped to a lamp post. She stopped to read it. The poem was also titled, but unsigned. She folded it, put in in her pocket and continued on her way.

That evening after class, she noticed another poem taped to a lamp post. She discovered it was another unsigned poem. All the poems were different. She pocketed the poem along with the the others and went on her way.

Then she saw someone several yards in front of

her taping something to a wall. He was dressed entirely in black, except for red boots. As the man left, she investigated what he had left behind. It was another unsigned poem.

She snatched the poem from the wall and began to follow the man in red boots. He was walking through a park. Then her phone rang, distracting her. She answered it.

"Hello? Oh hey listen, let me call you back. I'm busy at the moment. Later." She hung up and noticed that the poet was no longer in the park. She looked around, but couldn't find him. He was gone.

Upset over losing sight of the poet, she left the park and entered a small, cramped, dimly lighted bar. As her eyes adjusted to the darkness, she saw a couple paying their tab. She sat on a stool at the bar next to them and ordered a drink. She pulled one of the poems from her pocket and read it a second time. I almost got a glimpse of this person, this person's face, the poet himself, she thought. She cursed her phone for distracting her.

When the had couple left, and her eyes had adjusted to the darkness of the bar, she noticed someone sitting a few stools away, hunched over a drink. At first it did not seem like anyone at all — just a black shadow of a person. Then her eyes wandered down, and she saw the red boots.

She got up, holding her drink, and slowly walked toward him. She suddenly felt very nervous

"Excuse me," she said, in a tentative voice, bending down toward the poet, who turned his head up to look at her. Their eyes locked, his dark eyes on hers. He had short, slicked-black black hair, a trim black beard and mustache, and his skin was swarthy. He was stockily built. His eyes were like coal sacs, and his gaze was unwavering. He said nothing.

She said awkwardly, "Sorry, I hope I'm not bothering you, but I — I found these." She pulled the poems from her pocket, and set them down on the bar next to him. He looked down at them. Still he did not speak.

"I found them as I was walking today. I'm actually a writer myself. Well I try, anyway. But I just wanted to let you know that I think that they are really good."

The poet kept looking down at his poems, and then he looked back up at her. He spoke for the first time, his voice uninflected. "How did you know I wrote these?" he asked.

"Well, I saw you posting one, and I sorta followed you. I was sorta — curious — about you, and who would write these."

"You followed me to this bar?" he asked.

"No, I lost track of you when my phone went off. It's just a coincidence that I came in here."

The poet examined her. Her eyes. Her nervous hand gestures as she spoke.

"Why did you take these poems?"

"I really liked them and wanted to let you know."

"These poems are for everyone," the man said, with an angry edge to his voice. "Why would you just take them and why would you follow me? What would you know about poetry to just take them like that?" She could see that he was getting really angry, and stepped back from his hard, dark gaze.

"I'm sorry, I really am, I really didn't mean to offend you. It's just I really wanted to keep them, they're very good, and I didn't mean to follow you. I was just, well, I was just so curious as to who could write poems like these. I'm sorry. I'll leave you alone and leave you with your work."

As she turned to leave the poet got up. "Wait," he said. "I'm sorry." His voice had suddenly lost its anger. She turned back to look at him.

"You caught me off guard," he said. "No one really knows I do this. But thank you for appreciating my work. Here, keep these."

He handed her back the poems and she took them. "Thank you," the young woman said, with a nervous smile.

"Let me buy you a drink," the poet offered, his voice suddenly affable.

"Sure," she said, and took the stool next to his. When the drinks came she said, "I'm curious what your name is. All your poems are unsigned."

"My name is Maya."

34

"Maya. What an unusual name. I'm Arianna." As they reached to shake hands, she noticed that his hands had cuts on them and his nails were stained. They were dark, ruddy, working hands.

"Why," she asked, suddenly feeling bold, "do you post poems without your name, or any sort of contact information?"

The poet took a drink, thought for a moment, and then said, "I like to remain anonymous."

"Why?"

"Just seems like the appropriate way for me to express myself. I don't do well with attention. I never had it before so it makes me uncomfortable."

"So you have a lot of secrets, then?"

Maya nodded, looking down at his drink.

"If I tell you a secret, will you tell me one?" Arianna asked Maya.

She noticed that he hesitated. But then he said, "OK. Tell me your secret."

"My mother killed herself a year ago last week. I've never told anyone, not even my close friends."

Maya regarded her with dark, somber eyes.

"I'm sorry," he said, after a while.

"Thank you, Maya."

"Why don't you want to tell anyone?"

"I didn't really get along with her. I'm not sure if I'm even sad that she died." She gazed down into her drink and added, "But ever since she died, I've been having bad anxiety attacks. Like I can't sleep and I get really nervous."

She looked up at him, and saw he was looking at her. "Now you," she said.

"Well, I actually suffer from a severe anxiety disorder. I get anxiety and panic attacks. I've had them for years. I take meds and it helps but I still get them. So I understand you when you said you get them. I also never tell anyone either. That's why I write poems really. It helps me cope with my depression."

He hung his head in sadness. She laid a hand on his shoulder.

"Thanks," he said.

Later, Maya opened the door to his small, cramped studio apartment, turned on the light, and showed her in. There was a mattress covered in black without a bedstead, a desk, a chair, and a clutter of books, but little else. A small kitchen was in the rear. She offered to fix them drinks.

He sat on the bed and she sat on the only chair. They made a toast to poetry and then she said, mischief in her voice, "So, are you going to show me?"

"Show you what?"

"More of your poetry."

He reached for a white box, opened the lid, and handed it to her. "No one has seen these," he said.

Maya sat on the edge of the bed and watched her read. She read through them one by by one, turning over the pages as she did. From a couple of them she learned that he worked as a porter, cleaning bars, and often slept in them if he had to. It fit him, she thought, fit his burly build, his rough, scarred workman's hands. Finally she placed the poems neatly stacked back inside the box.

"These are amazing," she said.

"Thank you."

"Why don't you share them?"

Maya just shook his head.

"You need to share these. Like have a reading or show somewhere. ... Listen, Maya, I'm a college student, and I have a dissertation that I have due about writers. I would love to use your work. I can talk to Pratt. It's the university I attend. They can get a gallery and we can display your poems and you can recite some. We can make it public."

Maya took another drink. "I never went to college," he said, sounding vaguely regretful.

"Well, what do you say?" she asked.

After thinking it over he said: "I don't know if I really feel comfortable sharing my poems like that. I mean, I don't think people from Pratt would get them. You're the only one who does. I don't know if anyone else would. I don't want to be exposed like that."

"I won't expose you in a way that will make you feel uncomfortable," Arianna said, suddenly enthusiastic. "I just look at all these poems and I want everyone to feel the deepness and beauty in them. You will be helping me and I'll be helping you. This can probably lead to great things. You can probably even get a book of your poetry published. We can even work on one together."

Maya stood up, and began pacing back and forth in front of his bed. Maya noticed his hand shaking as he took another drink from his glass.

"Maya, are you OK? I'm not upsetting you, am I?"

Maya continued pacing, taking deep breaths. "I just feel overwhelmed right now," he said. He began breathing heavily and Arianna got up from the chair and approached him and sat him down on the bed and put her arm around him.

"I'm sorry if I overwhelmed you. I'm sorry. I just got really excited for you."

She began rubbing his back and put her head on his shoulder.

"I just want you to know that I think that this can be really good for you."

Maya began to calm down. He finished his drink and took a deep breath.

"You really think people will get it and not mock me?"

Arianna looked at him with sensitive eyes. "I won't let anyone do that to you."

Maya looked at her for a few seconds and then slowly nodded.

"OK. I'll do this for you." He extended his hand, his cut-up hand, toward her, and she took it. At that moment they heard a rumble of thunder, and a heavy rain began to pelt the pane of the apartment's only window.

"Shit," Maya said. "I didn't even know that it was supposed to rain and I don't have my umbrella in my backpack. And it's getting late."

"You could stay here for the night if you want," Maya told her.

"I wouldn't want to be a bother."

"It's not a bother. I'll take the floor and you can take the bed."

Arianna suddenly sat down on the edge of the bed and examined it. "We can share the bed," she said. "It won't bother me."

Maya hesitated, and then said, "OK."

They had a few more drinks until both were drowsy. It was dark outside, and the rain continued to pelt the pane. She took off her shoes and lay on the far end of the bed facing the wall. Maya took his boots off, set the alarm, and then lay on the opposite side of the bed, his back next to hers. As a flash of lightning lit up the room and thunder shook the window pane, Arianna began to rock back and forth on the bed, agitated. Maya turned and wrapped an arm around her to comfort her, and soon they both fell asleep as the rain slackened to a slight patter on the pane.

Maya's poems were set to make their debut in a gallery on the Lower East Side. Arianna arrived early with the owner of the gallery and her English professor.

"We promoted this show all over social media," her professor said. "Has your poet seen it?"

"He's not really a social-media kind of person," Arianna replied. "I'm lucky I convinced him to do this at all. He said he was doing it for me."

"A lot of people are excited about this," the gallery owner said. "This poet has been a mystery for years. Many people have found his anonymous poems and wondered who the writer was."

The professor took a glass of wine for himself, and handed another to Arianna. Then he said: "The world will finally get to meet this anonymous Beat poet, Arianna. This is going to look really good for you and your hard work at Pratt."

She regarded him with some skepticism. He went on: "I invited some of the city's top Instagram influencers. They are going to love him. Trust me, one photo with these people, and he is going to become social-media star."

As the gallery owner and the professor toasted each other in a self-satisfied way, Arianna looked at them with confusion, and growing unease.

Finally she told them: "Those aren't really the people that would understand what he has to say. I was really hoping to do this without all the added publicity. It's mostly for my fellow students and certain other people I invited, people who would understand."

"Oh, don't worry about it, Arianna, we're going to turn your friend into a star."

As the opening of the show neared, Arianna saw a line forming outside the gallery. She wasn't expecting so many people, and worried that they would make Maya uncomfortable. She began greeting the guests as they entered. She did not know most of them. Some people came in dressed as stereotypes of beatniks, wearing berets and sunglasses and taking pictures next to the framed poems rather then reading them. Arianna became increasingly anxious. People approached her to ask how she had discovered the poet. She responded uneasily, while watching the front door. Finally two unmistakable red boots strode in through the door. Seeing the large crowd, Maya immediately froze. She hurried over to him and guided him to a secluded corner of the gallery.

"Look Maya," she said, "there are a lot of people here, more than I expected, and a lot of them want to meet you. So if you feel uncomfortable please let me know. I'll stick by you for the whole evening, if you want."

Maya scanned the gallery, and noticed the way many people were dressed and how they were taking selfies in front of his framed poems.

"I can use a drink, actually," he told Arianna.

"Yes, let's get you a drink."

Arianna snatched Maya's hand to guide him through the crowd, but he yanked it away.

"You don't need to do that," he said curtly.

"Sorry," she said. "I was just trying to make you feel comfortable."

They got a couple of drinks, and then Arianna introduced him to her professor and the gallery owner.

"The poet himself, unmasked at last," the professor burbled with delight, while vigorously shaking Maya's hand. "You have great work here, son. Arianna tells me you never went to college."

"I couldn't afford to go." He yanked his hand back from the affable hand shaking it.

"Well, son, you have potential for college. There are some programs that can help you, help you financially if you need it."

Arianna observed at once that Maya looked insulted. The professor, meanwhile, was looking at him hopefully.

"Thanks," Maya said, "but I don't take charity."

"This is a huge show for you, Maya," the gallery owner said. "People are going to be talking about you after this."

Maya watched those taking selfies in front of his poems, wearing berets and sunglasses. He asked Arianna, "Why are people dressed like it's the 1950s?"

"I don't know. Probably because they think this is what poets look like."

"I don't dress like an idiot," Maya responded with contempt in his voice.

He helped himself to another drink, and as the night wore on and Arianna introduced him to various so-called admirers, his anxiety spiked and he began to drink heavily, grabbing drink after drink from a serving tray. Suddenly a random stranger walked up to him and said: "This is my first poetry show. How about you?" He wore a goofy smile.

Maya, drunk, tipsily studied the man. Finally he asked, "Have you actually read any of the poems?"

"Oh, no, I'm here with some influencers."

"What the hell," Maya demanded, are 'influencers'?"

"Oh, it's when people take pictures at events and put them online and they get notoriety and become like celebrities that can influence others. I plan to be an influencer myself."

Maya listened, speechless.

"Tonight isn't about you, or about the poetry. It's about the event! It's like — how did they put it back in the 60s? — a happening. And the hook is, we unmasked the anonymous poet at last! Don't you see?"

The man rambled on, but Maya looked at him with utter disgust and turned and walked away from him while he was still talking.

Arianna was trying to locate Maya in the crowd when the gallery owner stopped her.

"It's almost time for your poet to recite for us, Arianna, if you can introduce him to the audience."

She finally found him leaning against a wall in a corner with a drink in his hand. "Maya, they're ready for you to recite." She could tell he was drunk.

"I don't want to."

Arianna laid her hands on his shoulders and said, "I need you to do this for me. Everyone is ready to hear you. Please, Maya."

"They're not here for me." He shrugged her hands off of his shoulders, finished the drink and threw his glass to the floor. It broke into pieces.

"Maya please," she begged. Her voice sounded frantic. "Don't do it for me. Do it for you."

He thought about it, and finally nodded. "OK, I'll do it. But not for me. For you."

Arianna escorted him to the center of the gallery and approached the microphone.

"Hello everyone, and thank you for coming to this event. I would like to introduce to you the mystery man behind the words on the walls. His name is Maya."

The crowd burst into applause as Maya shuffled toward the microphone. Several people wearing berets and shades approached Maya. Just as drunk as he was, they began to shout and cheer and snap their fingers. "Like, yeah man!" one drunk shouted into his face. "Where are your bongos?" Arianna could tell that Maya was really angry. Someone yelled, "Like, you need to put these on, man," and threw a pair of sunglasses at Maya. They hit his chest, and fell to the floor. He looked down at them. People were laughing — they were laughing at him.

Maya bent down, retrieved the sunglasses from the floor, and put them on.

"You guys want me to wear these?" The crowd began to cheer.

"Do you people want to take pictures of me with these on?" The crowd cheered some more.

Maya began to laugh into the mic hysterically. Arianna's anxiety grew as he continued laughing. The harder he laughed, the quieter the crowd got until all you could hear was Maya's laughter. He stopped laughing and swept a hand at the subdued crowd.

"Let me ask you assholes in the front a question," he bellowed. "Why the fuck are you dressed like a bunch of fucking beatniks?"

Everyone was silent.

"I'm not a fucking beatnik and my poems are not backgrounds for your fucking selfie pics. Fuck off!"

Maya yanked off the shades and threw them back into the crowd. He then stalked over to his framed poems and tore them from the walls, one after another. The gallery owner tried to stop him, laying a hand on him. Maya pushed the hand off of him and yelled at the man, "These are mine, not yours, and if you touch me again I'll break one of these frames over your fucking head." The gallery owner backed away in fear, and then Maya stalked out of the gallery to stunned silence, his liberated poems sticking out of his pants pockets and his red boots slapping violently on the floor.

Arianna, overwhelmed, darted out of the gallery in pursuit of Maya. She spotted the drunken poet staggering on the sidewalk just ahead of her.

"Maya, wait," she screamed. He turned and gave her the finger and continued walking. The gesture shocked her, but she chased after him anyway, caught up with him and stopped him.

"Maya what happened? Why did you do that?"

Maya whirled angrily upon her and yelled into her face: "Are you following me again? You fucking lied to me! You told me that people would get it. No one did! All they did was take photos and dressed like idiots. I trusted you with the only things that I have, my poems, and you exploited them and me."

Arianna burst into tears.

"I didn't invite those people," she protested. "I had no idea that they were going to show up till right before the show started. I just wanted to help you, and now because of your drunken outburst, I might fail."

"You wanted to help me?" Maya hissed at her. "Well, here, then." Maya threw a framed poem onto the sidewalk. "Take that poem. Take it! And then never speak to me again. I never want to see you again. I never should have trusted you."

Maya turned on his heels and stalked off, red boots stomping on the pavement. Arianna, still weeping, yelled, "I'm sorry!" She yelled into the street, "I'm sorry!" After a time she slipped the fragile page of poetry out of its shattered frame, smoothed and pocketed it. She remained on her knees weeping until he professor came to her aid.

After the disaster at the gallery, she lost all contact with Maya.

One evening many months later, Arianna passed a Lower East Side bar with a sign in front that read, "Poetry reading by Maya tonight."

She froze, and gazed down at the sign for a long time. She thought and thought.

Finally she went in.

The bar was packed with people waiting to see and hear Maya read. She navigated her way through the dense crowd to the bar and ordered a drink. As she waited for it she overheard someone say, "Hey, there's the the chick who put on his first show, when he flipped out. I saw her face on Instagram, all about that disaster."

Her ears burned. When the drink came, she took a quick gulp.

With her hand shaking so violently that the ice rattled in the drink, she went in search of a free seat around the small lighted stage. None were to be found. It was a standing-room-only crowd. Finding a narrow opening against the wall, she watched as the host approached the mic on stage and bellowed into it: "Ladies and gentlemen, let's give it up for Maya!"

Maya, dressed entirely in black except for his trademark red boots as always, mounted the stage and moved behind the mic. Everyone applauded wildly. Maya thanked them with a bow, and then began to read. He began to read a poem entitled, "New York I have no where else to go." Arianna felt her breath hitch, and her eyes got big. It was the very first poem of his that she had found and read, the one that had been taped to a trash can.

Maya began the second verse when he happened to look up, in her direction, his head pulled there as if by some invisible, providential force. Their eyes locked for a second. He hesitated in his reading, causing an uncomfortable rustle among the crowd. Then he looked down and resumed reading hurriedly: "New York I have nowhere else to be a working stiff and a late-night drinker."

Arianna recited the poem aloud, along with Maya.

After the show Maya greeted his fans, signed flyers, and even smiled. They were his audience, his people. Arianna, feeling a bit nervous, sidled up to him.

"Hi," she said.

"Hi."

"That was a wonderful reading, Maya."

He looked at her, then, the way he had first looked at her, with his heavy, dark, unsmiling gaze — the time she had first introduced himself.

But then he smiled.

"Thank you," he said simply. "I'm getting a drink. Would you like one?"

"Sure."

"Meet you at the table by the bar."

"OK."

He returned with the drinks and sat down next to her.

"So how've you been, Maya?" she asked him.

"Good. Doing a lot of writing. Wrote a novel. Waiting to hear back from an agent I sent it to."

"Wow, amazing! Good luck." She added, "It looks like your poems are actually being appreciated by the crowd you want."

"Yeah. It feels good." After a pause he added, "You know, I feel bad the way I overreacted that night. It didn't help that I got really drunk and made a scene. I'm sorry, Arianna."

"It's OK. I think about that night too. And of you."

Maya looked at Arianna. His breathing got labored,

and his hands shook. She knew what was happening, and leaned forward to hug him.

"I'm sorry," Maya whispered.

Arianna got down on one knee and rested her head on his lap and held his hand to calm him down.

"It's going to be OK, Maya," she told him. "I won't leave you."

The people around them were talking among themselves. Arianna stayed alongside Maya as he began to calm down. Her eyes were teary as she rested her head on his lap and held his hand.

At that moment they were calm together.

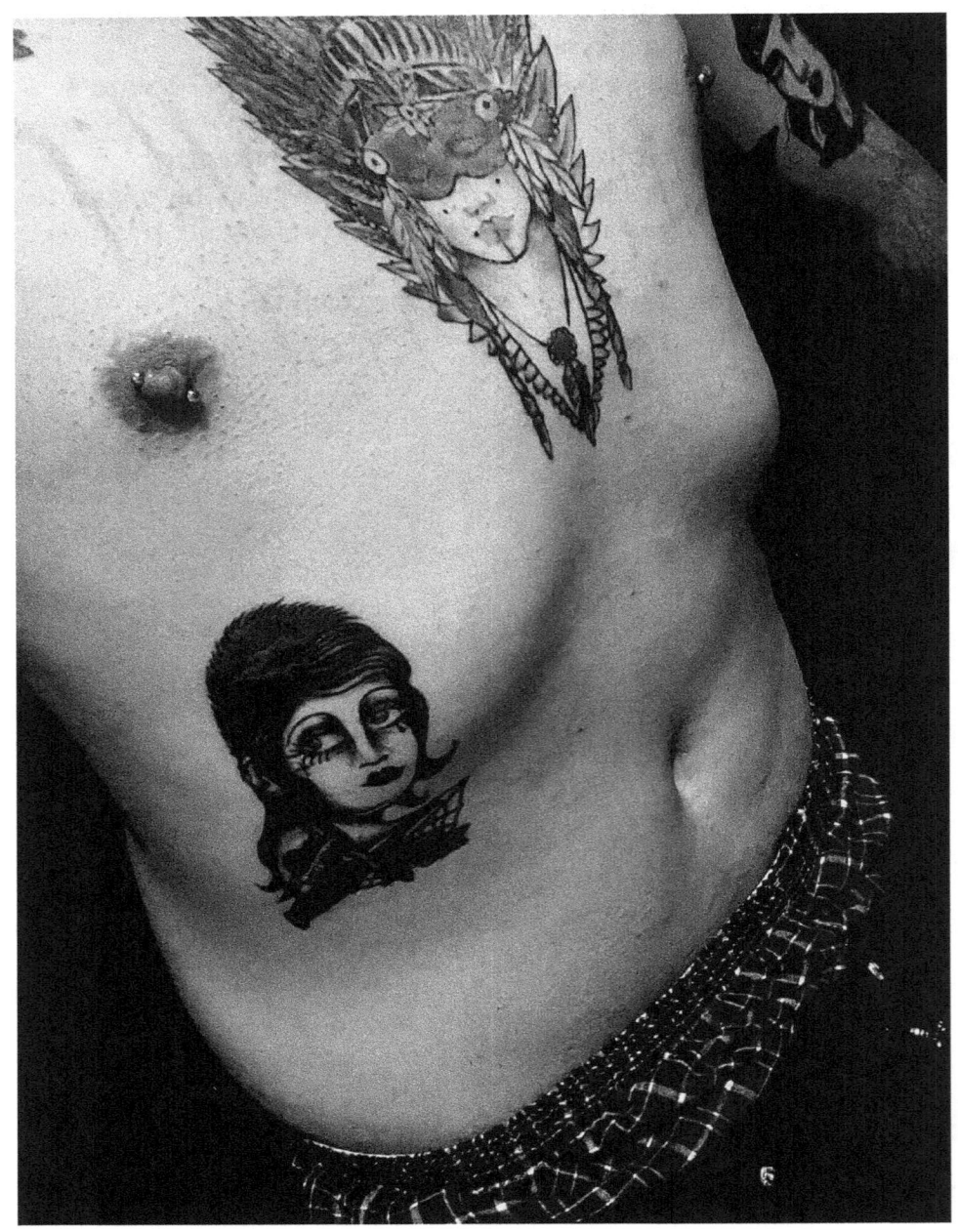

Damaged.

I do have something to live for. Just don't know what it is yet
maybe I'm not supposed to
it's not the aging that scares me. Or who will die next or last
or waiting in the cold on York St
maybe it's not having anything to write about the next day
or being damaged
damaged we are. The whole lot of us

Drugs #4-30-15

I'm clean Mr heroin
I broke up with coke so I can have a relationship with
whiskey
heavily medicated
pins and needles.

Best friends.

I know you've been having a rough time lately. Just wanted to remind you that I'm here for you because we are best friends.

Do you have a minute? I know you're in a hurry to be somewhere but, we are best friends,

but I want to be more then that.

When we finish each other's sentences we both crack up.

We can be goofy together and not have a care.

When one of us is thinking about the other, we reach for our phones at the same time.

When you are going home after a fun evening I won't go to sleep until you let me know you made it back safe.

You've been my shoulder to lean on, and I, your listener.

When you are not feeling like yourself I always try to find a way to make you smile.

And when you do smile I smile back at you and melt deep inside.

I would rather spend an entire day listening to your stories than doing anything else.

I would rather just gaze at you and in a good way forget about my day because I have your eyes to look at.

When we say goodbye for the night we hug. But now I don't want to let go.

Distress.

Her jewelry was made of bones. Decay was her style.

It was nice to see you again Vicki.

It's snowed two days before and you couldn't even tell
It all disappeared so fast
Only when I bumped into you is when I realized it
It was awkward but I wouldn't have had it any other way
The construction is almost done you know
No excuses for not wanting to come see me as I'm not there to be seen
I no longer have a reflection that I can blame
No damaged hand to hold
No tearful eyes to stare into
Now I just cough up Rorschach's
The time is an hour ahead
And there's no more water to drink
Just a shot of, I don't know. I'd rather not say
The mass is in C minor
Kissed lips are now blue
The smell of a Catholic Church
Something is burning below Grand St
And my vision is zero.

Cocktail of the month.

Summer's here finally. But two more weeks of spring would have been nice
2 weeks of giving lovely tourists paper flowers
foreign languages are lovely in the summer
with green eyes
a foreign tongue
a french post card
New York is great for holidays
so is Berlin
history painted on the streets
paper flowers and a drink that's poured but not there
It's summer now
spring left yesterday
before the dying hour
holidays are celebrated separately.

Pitchers of lilies.

**The time has come to move on
the lilies have spoken for me
they want to bloom elsewhere
four years was so long ago
roses die with beauty
lilies rot
They are kept in the dark. It's safer there
It's what they know best
there's beauty elsewhere.**

A cold breeze in May.

The clouds began to hide the sun in Cobble Hill

it was two weeks before my last notice and the winter wasn't quite over

and in the middle of the day I thought of an intimate encounter that had happened days before

the last time I sweated. I spent the evening with my friend with colorful tattoos

it was our last evening together in the same room

the breeze was still out when I told her that I would miss getting her coffee and thanked her for the two years of everything

the breeze was gentle with the leaves on the tree that were in my view. Like running your fingers through long hair

I wrote about that tree I told myself

I've seen that tree die and come back to life

May is an interesting time to change your life.

It's an interesting time to feel the breeze and to say farewell.

Done And Done.

    A pretty face and a pouring glass with a light that reflects from both eyes and candle

    Like a kaleidoscope with every shade that sound's round and round

    Round and round
And around and around

    With every shade a stained glass

    A "biblical" kind of color blind

    That goes around and around

    Slowly this time

    Around and around

Press Eject.

      Press eject to release the muffled recordings
An engraved forearm

      Press eject

      If you want to hear the iron green door close

      Press eject

      For the gift-wrapped sparrow skull
The fragrance of a theater

      A daughter from a man who's grand

      Press eject

      The haunted echoes of a statue

      An effigy

      Press eject

      Heavy machinery

      Green arrows crossed

      Press reject.

Bonne Nuit.

Why won't you show yourself?

Is it the years that have passed?

The time difference?

My tongue is not a language barrier

I'm aging myself

In a bad way

The downtown surge that has taken away my fiends

And the ones before that

The greeting in a foreign tongue

It should've been me as I say every day

I can't stand to look at my own image in the mirror that has no curtain to hide me from it.

Just a stain of dried-up sorrows

Do you ever ask yourself "if only you were here?"

My thoughts have become my personal motto

A paradox

Toward the parallel lines facing midtown

>   **The Latin of Manhattan**

>   **Every day is the last day on earth**

>   **You would have adored him**

>   **Good morning and good night.**

DUMBO.

Down under the Manhattan bridge overpass the cobblestone streets are still there and the warehouses still have painted advertisements of days past

Mermaids swim on the arch of the bridge and poems are written in the pathways where old New York hears them and remains old New York, old New Yorker walking along the bridge where I fell in love and will never forget

Ephedrine in the Japanese art space where the crazy Russian with beautiful eyes is crazier than I'll ever be. She runs in the snow in the nude. I've always wanted her

Down on Jay Street the angel faced cherub serves me. The exotic one listens to my stories her eyes as strong as Ireland's harp

Plymouth St is where the piano keys are heard from afar and letters for future encounters are ignored delivered by the dapper tramp

The east river battle fields are gardens now

**And the five points can be seen from there
The drinks taste better on 68 Jay**

Eyes as strong as county cork you know?

A poem by Feo.

    Has it been 12 years?

    Has it been that long since I was jailed in Clinton St with only 2 delis across from each other where I used to spend my tips?

    Has it been 12 years since I started wearing paisley ties?

    Has it been 12 years that I just pretended to know what I was doing?

    Has it been that long since I ended up in a Brooklyn hospital?

    Has it been that long since I woke up and said fuck it?

    It's been that long since the French woman was on her own too.

    Well time doesn't fly

    It wakes up every morning not knowing how it got here.

Deep - Nerval.

Go get dressed and do something violent
Kiss the sidewalk
Lick the wounds
Set off smoke alarms in the small villages near Corona
Play with danger
There's a ghost off Halsey, staring out into magic land
Her walk has disappeared by now.

Dear mother,

I am writing to you from my new job here in America.

I hope that you haven't been too worried but I promised myself that I wouldn't write until I found work.

So far America has been good to me. I got a room in Queens that a friend of mine back home helped me get. It's not much but at least I have something.

I'm still trying to figure my way around the trains. It can be difficult, especially late at night. I have to make sure I catch the train on time otherwise it changes lines and I get very confused.

I got a job at a restaurant cleaning and washing dishes. I'm going to take english classes so I can get a better position as a server. Someone there is going to help me get a second job renovating apartments in Brooklyn, so that should keep me busy.

America is a very fascinating place. Especially New York. There are people here from all over the world and the country. I met my first Jewish person, a woman who I work with.

When I have free time I explore. I went to Coney Island and saw the Atlantic Ocean.

I walked the Brooklyn Bridge and saw the statue of liberty. Just like the immigrants before me. I took a picture that I will send to you.

Sometimes I really like riding the trains. I stare out at all the buildings, the different neighborhoods, and the flags from other countries that fly from apartment windows. The view of Manhattan from my train ride to work is such a beautiful view.

I do get lonely here sometimes. Even though I'm surrounded by millions, I still don't know anyone. It's taking time to get used to everything, but I do feel safer here than I do back home.

I have to get back to work. I promise to write back soon. Love you mother. I hope one day you can come visit me and see the statue of liberty, and the view of the city from the train.

Shameless last words.

He once told the truth, and paid dearly for it
He knows no appreciation in the late season
Art is made best when the hands are sad
Alcohol sweats from my forehead to my eyes
The cracked American
The lucky jester
Under a glass spell
An imprinted circle
The bottle is empty and broken.

The ugly generation.

There's a lot of potholes in New York
The streets are broken
Late at night when the drunks are out, buildings are knocked down and the scaffolding goes up
But no one cares
14th St is a maze in orange and white and graffiti
There's traps set in there, for the junkies to rent
Heroin will never leave the streets of New York
Aging East Village punks are dying a slow death of unwanted change
There's no methadone for that
There is only luxury billboards and tattooed fortunes
Brooklyn isn't the only one that's dying a slow death
Aren't we all
The addiction has taken over every burrough that I've been through
And there's not enough on my metro card to do it twice
What ever happened to the poor family in Brooklyn?
Can I rest my head on your shoulder?
Life can be difficult
But dying is a breeze
I will be spread across the Brooklyn Bridge cause I want to have the best view
Let me ask you, do sober people fall in love?
I do
Many hearts are broken on the express train
Debris ruins my writing on windy days
But every once in awhile someone finds it
An ugly New York poem can change everything, like crying in public
The Lower East Side in autumn nights
The comfort of misery
Floating above Manhattan and getting home sick for Chinatown
Fuggedubadit! Vito says. The last Italian on Mulberry
A call is made once every 6 months, to remind you that I care
Once every 3 years I confess love, and lose her forever
My muse is here to believe in me
That's how much New York loves you
We will drown for you

Or float
Your namesake is in there and I want you
Both of youse.
Don't want to lose you Manhattan
Yo Queens, take care of mom will ya?
Fucking amateurs
They've never cried in public
There bodies have never been bruised
They don't know how to bleed the way we do
That's the difference
They're new to this
And we're the ugly generation.

Feo

Who is that masked man? He's a New York City poet and photographer, and this is his third book. His first, The Light Fantastic, was recently published, along with The Bar is Open, both by Pood Paw Prints. Photos in this book are by Feo.

David Misialowski

Is a published New York City fiction writer, poet, and professional artist. He worked for 18 years as a staff editor on The New York Times. Since leaving The Times, he has reverted to his standard role as a curmudgeonly misanthrope. He is the editor of this volume.

Other Books by Pood Paw Prints:

The Pood: Michigan's Inferno
Pantheon: Heterotopia
Pantheon: Heterothanasia
Pantheon: HeteroGenia
Abe 2.0: Welcome to the Asylum, Mr President
Eternity Invasion
The Light Fantastic by Feo
The Bar is Open by Feo

www.poodpawprints.com
facebook.com/poodpawprints
youtube.com/@poodpawprints
instagram.com/poodpawprints

Scott Thorson

Publisher.
Published Author.
Dancing girl on Thursdays.
Knows Liberace from film.
Watching to see if you are good or bad. He knows.
Can't rhyme word things.

www.ingramcontent.com/pod-product-compliance
Lightning Source LLC
Chambersburg PA
CBHW071416040426
42444CB00009B/2268